LIFE WATCH

ALSO BY WILLIS BARNSTONE

Poetry

Poems of Exchange   1951
From This White Island   1960
A Day in the Country (for children)   1971
New Faces of China   1973
China Poems   1976
Overheard   1979
A Snow Salmon Reached the Andes Lake   1980
Ten Gospels & a Nightingale   1981
The Alphabet of Night   1984
Five A.M. in Beijing   1987
Funny Ways of Staying Alive   1993
The Secret Reader • 501 Sonnets   1996
Algebra of Night: New & Selected Poems (1948-98)   1999

Translations

The Other Alexander (Greek novel by Margarita Liberaki)   Foreword by Albert Camus (with
   Helle Tzalopoulou Barnstone)   1959
Greek Lyric Poetry   1961
Sappho: Poems in the Original Greek with a Translation   1965
The Poems of Saint John of the Cross   1968
The Poems of Mao Tse-Tung (with Ko Ching-Po)   1972
My Voice Because of You: Pedro Salinas   Preface by Jorge Guillén   1976
A Bird of Paper: Poems of Vicente Aleixandre   Preface by Vicente Aleixandre   1982
Laughing Lost in the Mountains: Poems of Wang Wei (with Tony Barnstone & Xu Haixin)
   1991
Six Masters of the Spanish Sonnet   1993
To Touch the Sky: Poems of Mystical, Spiritual & Metaphysical Light   1999
The New Covenant: Four Gospels and Apocalypse   2002
Border of a Dream: The Poems of Antonio Machado   2003

Literary Criticism

The Poetics of Ecstasy: From Sappho to Borges   1983
The Poetics of Translation: History, Theory, Practice   1993

Memoirs

With Borges on an Ordinary Evening in Buenos Aires   1993
Sunday Morning in Fascist Spain: A European Memoir (1948-1953)   1995

Anthologies / Editions

Modern European Poetry   1967
Eighteen Texts: Contemporary Greek Authors (with Edmund Keeley)   1973
Concrete Poetry: A World View (with Mary Ellen Solt)   1974
A Book of Women Poets from Antiquity to Now (with Aliki Barnstone)   1980
Borges at Eighty: Conversations   1982
The Other Bible: Ancient Alternative Scriptures   1984
Literatures of Asia, Africa, and Latin America (with Tony Barnstone)   1999
The Gnostic Bible (with Marvin Meyer)   2003

LIFE WATCH

Poems by

WILLIS BARNSTONE

AMERICAN POETS CONTINUUM SERIES, NO. 77

BOA Editions, Ltd. ✥ Rochester, NY ✥ 2003

First Edition
03 04 05 06 7 6 5 4 3 2 1

Publications by BOA Editions, Ltd.—
a not-for-profit corporation under section 501 (c) (3)
of the United States Internal Revenue Code—
are made possible with the assistance of grants from
the Literature Program of the New York State Council on the Arts,
the Literature Program of the National Endowment for the Arts,
the Sonia Raiziss Giop Charitable Foundation,
the Lannan Foundation,
as well as from the Mary S. Mulligan Charitable Trust,
the County of Monroe, NY,
Ames-Amzalak Memorial Trust,
and The CIRE Foundation.

See Colophon on page 144 for special individual acknowledgments.

Cover Design: Daphne Poulin-Stofer
Cover Photo: Rick Becker-Leckrone
Interior Design and Composition: Richard Foerster
Manufacturing: McNaughton & Gunn, Lithographers
BOA Logo: Mirko

NATIONAL
ENDOWMENT
FOR THE ARTS

State of the Arts

NYSCA

Library of Congress Cataloging-in-Publication Data

Barnstone, Willis, 1927-ed.
    Life watch / Willis Barnstone.
        p. cm.--(American poets continuum series; no. 77)
    ISBN 1-929918-36-4 (alk. paper)
        I. Title. II. American poets continuum series; v. 77

PS3503.A6223L542003
811'.54--dc21

                                                          2003044302

BOA Editions, Ltd.
Steven Huff, Publisher
H. Allen Spencer, Chair
A. Poulin, Jr., President & Founder (1938–1996)
260 East Avenue, Rochester, NY 14604
www.boaeditions.org

for my father and the lonely reader

CONTENTS

Dawn Café

Train to Paris

LIFE WATCH

Train to Paris

The Farewell

I picked this sprig of heather
Autumn is dead recall our fate
On earth we'll never see each other
Smell of time sprig of heather
And remember for you I wait

—Guillaume Apollinaire (1881–1918)

TRAIN TO PARIS

In the night boat train
from Le Havre to Paris
I sit by a young woman my age
who is from Carpentras,
daughter of a Breton sculptor,
and we are heartsick
after our three hours. We know
we'll never meet again
except she will remember
me, our hands, and I her,
though I learn in 1956,
four years after our night,
she died on a Paris street
when a car crushed her
from behind. In her grave
we are sitting cramped
but our conversations never
run out of gravity.
Down from the train of time
(I piss on time), we endure as souls
and our scandals create us
on the platform kissing.

GAS LAMP, 1893

In brownstone Boston down on old Milk Street,
up two gray flights, near the gas lamp, the tailor
waits glumly for the midwife. August heat
has worn the woman out. Amid the squalor
she looks around the bed, clutching a cape
she brought from London as a child. It's dawn
and dirty. The dark tailor wants to escape
to his cramped shop. The woman's sheets are drawn
below her waist. She isn't hollering now.
Her eyes are dark and still; blood on her thumbs.
Her name is Sarah. No. I'm guessing. How,
untold, am I to know? Hot day has worn
into the room. The midwife finally comes.
Grandmother bleeds to death. My father's born.

IN OUR LIFE WATCH

In our life watch we are down to five
or six Pierre Grange watches, a jeweler's box
of soft Swiss straps and a few
precious stones we are selling off to pay
the Greystone Hotel bill and meals.

Dad and I leave early each morning
on our rounds in the labyrinths
of narrow jewelry stores downtown.
How will we eat after our loot is gone? No worry.
Some way. I love this summer in New York,

best in my life. Not Camp Modin in Maine
with its daybreak lake and canoe trips
but real city watch shops with grownup men
we waylay and haggle with. On Sunday
we prowl Coney Island or the World's Fair.

Dad was twelve when he left home and school.
I'll soon be twelve and I've got
my father as my closest pal. We celebrate
each sale, each trade. One afternoon
with a twinkle he slaps down 300 bucks

for a diamond—most of what we have
to live on. Next day sells it for a thousand.
He finds the way. Things get so good
we spend our Sundays watching Gehrig
and DiMaggio knocking leather into the bleachers

or Peewee Reese catching the impossible.
We miss the Series when dad goes West
but I grab wartime trains to meet him
on our swinging life watch through red
mountain states and Mexico adventures.

In Mexico City he marries a child bride
and I'm living with Spanish children
from the civil war in a barred-in orphanage
where I share a room on the roof.
Then, too soon, dad and I talk all night

in our New York hotel. Lying on narrow beds,
we conjure up Rembrandt's beggar in baggy
nobleman's dress, how the Swedish Angel
wrestler hugs a foe till he drops inert.
Then the hill of debts. Am I father tonight?

In the morning I leave for Maine,
he's on a plane to Mexico where he must
pawn his soul for silver. No luck.
He flies to Colorado, plays a last card
at a Denver bank. Loses. Van Gogh's face

against the wall, he climbs high to the roof
where he folds his coat, places it
on a stone bench near the ledge, his hat on top.
He steps over the low railing, leaps,
and floats in blind sorrow out into May sun.

Dad's fallen again, but we can't wake early
and look up a small jewelry shop
to peddle our wares and hearts,
our soft Swiss straps or cold diamond,
since death at last has cleaned us out.

Room of the orphans

After my father's suicide, young Marti,
    my Mexican stepmother,
goes back to the iron bed with her mother
    Rebeca, a Sefardí
from Constantinople, who normally
    calls me *mancebito*,

young man (in medieval Spanish),
    but she is afraid I'll get
her daughter as my father had.
    They rent some rooms behind
the great cathedral, a small hovel
    in the old district. I too

live this year in Mexico City,
    near Marti, in an orphanage.
If I can't make it back by ten
    (I give evening classes
all over the city to earn some pesos)
    I do an all nighter,

reading in a lowdown café, or better,
    go to Marti's and sleep
on a straw mat on the floor
    between the tiny Indian maid
and her brother Sam, an army captain.
    Often when I am broke

I sell my blood in a clinic, and on
    one Saturday twice—but not
in the same place. The nurse
    notices the fresh pricks
but she lets me through. Beautiful Marti
    is only two years older than me

and before my father made his move
she was my first date.
I care for her and never know
that the mere sale
of my blood is for her a stigma
God will not forgive

but who could not forgive us for
necking in the backseat
of Dad's Buick. In the morning
when my train pulls out,
she gives me a silk handkerchief
painted with a red guitar.

FIXING THE LIFE WATCH

My cousin Harold in French-speaking Maine,
where I was born, is humped over the seat
by the store window, looking at our Seine—

the Androscoggin Falls where waters beat
on great black rocks in this Canuck town. Jacques,
Jean Pierre and dad are kids who like to cheat

the angel death by hanging from a steel track
on which the freight trains grumble overhead.
Then they dive into the foam and swim back

up to coal wagons lingering on the spread
of gleamy rails. Hal repairs the mainspring
of busted watches, loupe on his forehead,

his eye bloating the lens, his mind brimming
with semiprecious jewels and caves of pins
where only tiny tools can heal a broken wing

of steel into a singing wheel. Dad sins
with lovers. Harold turns the screws. Then dad
begins to import watches and he wins

Dora's green heart. A lot of hearts go mad
or break; some are tossed out. I never learn
to fix a watch or heart, and while I'm sad

that Hal, my dad and Dora now sojourn
under a Seine of sullen mud, I hear
them swimming close. Always stroking, they turn,
their voices floating faces to my ear.

AGAIN AT THE DENVER AIRPORT, RECALLING FEDERICO AND MY FOLKS IN 1929 IN NEW YORK

Seventy years ago Federico the poet from Granada sees
the Hudson from his desk on the seventh floor of John Jay Hall
at Columbia where he composes an exploding city.

He sees the Stock Exchange become a pyramid of moss
and a Chinese caterpillar emerge from the cocoon
of the new moon to swim as a monarch butterfly

over Brooklyn Bridge. There he pals with Hart Crane
in the Bronx where nuns proudly wear tattoos next
to their aluminum crosses. He sings *cante jondo,*

types in solitude. His lover is drinking his blood,
olive trees faint before black-caped Civil Guards
and gypsy Preciosa plays her parchment moon,

spinning a fish of eternity. In cricket autumn he trains
up through New England penumbra with a free ticket
to the mills of Lake Eden in Vermont where he foxtrots

with two old dignified American ladies in the cabin
they've restored with their own hands in the woods.
Then back from bears and syrup, he wanders with sailors

and an Assyrian hound who howls through black glass.
In 1962 in Madrid I am hours with Rosales the Falangist
friend who hid Lorca up in his attic near the police station

in Granada until the afternoon the firmament of Spain
collapses in hot coffee—meaning hot lead—and out
of equal madness Lorca is handcuffed to an anarchist

bullfighter and school teacher, trucked to a night ravine
by the Moorish *Well of Poison* outside his city, and shot
in the heart and the ass. In Colorado I read his New York letters

to his parents, saying, "I've high grades in English class.
Please send my allowance to Mister Federico García."
In 1929 when he walks from his room to the Hudson,

Bob and Blondie Barnstone live nearby on the Drive,
close to the glorious marble Soldiers and Sailors Monument
and wordless steel Joan of Arc, sex dream of my youth,

on her horse, facing the English skies of Manhattan,
with her spear raised toward heaven. If my dad, buried
near this airport in his adopted highlands, can meet

the poet in Morningside Heights, what will he say
to the Spaniard as they share a cab? Dad's never known
a poet, but he recites Poe's "Annabelle Lee" to me

in his baritone voice: "And I will lie down by my bride."
I wish he could tell you that his son Guillermo
(I am not yet two) will pass fifty years haunted by

your dream stallions, will steal your qasidas and ghazals
of a thousand Persian ponies asleep on a moonlit brow
and enraged riders pounding the drum of the plain

to their city where lanterns fail and pepper trees faint . . . .
I write you, Federico, from our own frontier, from this plane
now diving toward Sioux Falls, South Dakota, with only

white faces, starched farm lips of women who wear jeans
on their breasts and men beefy with iron belts and grins.
Oh, Federico, if you can know these north pampas of snow,

you'll walk hearty in your one hundred second year,
using an Arab cane, a carnation, and eyes of black jade
to pierce these Badlands and devise your last drama

of the youth choked with a gong of broken moons
in a bloody wedding with the fish of darkness and sand . . .
there your fingers spin forever, playing a child dead!

BACK IN 1901

Outdoors, cows and a Vermont barn. Inside
our eighteenth-century summer farmhouse,
I quit sanding and oiling wide pine floorboards

and show up back in 1901 in Boston, determined
to know my dad's father, whom I never saw.
On Milk Street, a ghetto named for a London

Milk Street ghetto, I find the lowdown
tenement where the choleric tailor lives
with a black woman, his common law wife.

The building stinks pleasantly of fried liver
and fish aromas sitting like tired old men
on the stairs I climb now like a regular.

Morris Bornstein heard of me from son Robert
but we were a century apart, he in New England,
I off upper Broadway. I knock. It's good

to knock on the unknown, on a nonentity
who may star in the story about the dog
who dreamt heaven in a butcher shop,

which no one yet cares to write about.
Grandfather opens. "Hello, I'm Billy," I say.
"No," he answers. I notice the immigrant English,

a wet shtetl lilt mixed with the Boston r that goes
unheard. "No," he insists. "If you are gray
and Robert's boy, then I am dead.

You can't be Billy!" "You're right," I apologize.
"*You* are dead and I am dreaming you."
At once I am ashamed. This is my ancestor,

ghettoized and despised by Poles, who steamered
over the sea from Warsaw to a Boston life
I couldn't guess. "I was kidding, Zeda,

I'm not even born, but I wanted to tell you
I love you." "You love me? You're a numbskull!"
And he kisses me. I think we're doing fine,

yet know I can't get out of these false tenses
and the small shop where his irons,
heating up on a wood stove, are owls looking

at me with contempt. I apologize again. "Sorry,
I've come so late to talk. I never wished to be cruel,
but you were gone when I was a child.

They never told me. So I fashioned your lips,
your Tartar eyes and crooked back,
your wife who isn't home yet. I mean, the maid."

"I don't get you, Billy." He lets go of my hand.
"Stay with me a while. I'm pretty happy."
I sit with him all night. In the morning Zeda gives me

a jacket he made, and presses it with special care.
When did he do it? We were awake together.
I take it. I'm descending slow stairs

smelling of Morris's shop, his owl irons, his glare.
Tonight I'm wearing the meticulously stitched
jacket, though it is tight and I'm a crummy actor.

FATHER

Dad, you are the first to choose the underworld,
so I spend most of my life chatting
with you down in your airless condo
with its old fashioned walls of coffin wood
your young wife and I select in Colorado Springs

where an afternoon in May,
when the lark sings and nightingale responds,
you leap wingless, envy of cursing gulls,
only to smash against the street.
Then the shrewd beauty and sorrow

that mingle a body and soul
break while your spirit flees and your corpse
lingers in a box that is soon dropped
with a terrible thud made of silence
for your one-way voyage into the pit.

Ah, father, you wait over a half century
for me to come down. I'm with the light still.
I like it here. Galaxies are out of reach,
but those winking ghosts of fire and gas
salt the night with our mystery seconds.

Now trapped in your solitary prison
(unimaginably black and soundless)
I wish you could have another twenty in bright air.
Why don't we go to Italy for gnocchi,
for brown-outlined faces on Sienna walls?

Speak up, dad. It is sad for me to play
your role, be you talking through me.
You give me bravery, say keep my shoulders back,
and this sunless afternoon, slouching,
I suddenly pop out of my chair to grab you.

Your profession is time and you design
a cosmopolitan watch to sell in shops.
I keep this Bauhaus life watch for us.
I keep you dead awake, and while I sleep
I hear us talk and pry open the dial.

A CHILD'S CHRISTMAS IN MANHATTAN

I snap a photo of the soul. It comes
out bedlam blue, reaching the snowball sky
of childhood where we are cutthroat bums
at ice war. Kids smack iceballs in your eye.
We blinded sledders burn way down the snow
gully, swerving a skid away from the third rail
sizzling deadly behind a barrier low
over the Hudson River's poisoned pail
of dead fish, condoms, and gray battleships
chatting of war in Asia. In our snow war
I take my hits on the way up. I duck
and fling my bombs. My frozen nose and lips
get whacked. Holy night, soul in Labrador,
I limp to mom's supper to get unstuck.

OUR NEW YORK SKYLINE IN THE 1930S, NOW ON FIRE IN SEPTEMBER

We faced the park and sometimes a big swan
over Manhattan rose from the small lake
where I went with my dad to row and scan
the New York skyline. Once a year mom took
a glass filled with pale wax and lit the wick,
her hands hovering over it like a well
she fell into. She wasn't weird or sick
but I didn't get it and broke her spell
with kid talk. Whispering for her dead, a Jew
on a few days, she never could parade
her feelings. Tonight I got myself to stand on
the street recalling mom's tall skyline that
had no Twin Towers then, nor now. Some prayed.
I slipped out awkwardly alone. All I could do
was let a candle burn out for those gone—
a girl in the plane flaming where she sat.

DASHING NORTH

My brother tells us, "Mother's on the train."
We leave Grand Central Station about ten,
rumbling, and should by dawn hit dazzling Maine
where she was born and where she'll go again
to lie forever. There are four of us,
two brothers and the wives, less permanent
than she who now—after the flight from Greece,
the canceled dream of southern France, the scent
of truffles near our city where we planned
to winter, after the botched operation—
lies by herself somewhere back a few cars
in her own box in which her sixty years
no longer dream. After we reach the station:
skullcaps and prayers and her light lost in sand.

MOTHER

Mother, isn't it time we had a meal
together? I'll run to the kitchenette
in our two rooms over Central Park,

bring the dishes to the card table
we set up for meals, and you let me know
what it's been like as bones locked

in a Maine coffin. Best if you could
whisper how you met dad in Auburn,
and how you felt when you and he,

in formal dress, handsome forever,
lay on the grass, on your elbows,
ready to conquer even the new moon

of later pain, you on sunwhite sheets
in Beth Israel, the shark of sorrow
sleeping you forever into the foam

of anaesthesia, your green eyes locked
as wild pancreatic white cells close
your brief life. I want to fill you in

on every dumb passion, and we need
at least a month just to get both
of us timed in the same photo

before you hop back to the grave.
I'll call to swing it so at last you are
paroled from the earth's indignity.

I'll do the dishes (better than I used to).
Then we'll walk about the city, dressed in
a special sun made for our yellow steps,

and when dusk hits our windows facing
the pond and swans in the sky, we'll eat
a sour cream and herring supper, put on slow

Valentino tango. You'll drop your reserve
as we sweep blind around the big Persian rug
whose peacock wings hug the night.

BROTHER

My brother, I want not only your company
and you to say, "Let's get in a wagon and shoot down
      to Belize or Zacatecas"
but a decade more together in global air
and your fingers creating beauty with black steel
      containing glass walls.

When you chose to live underground in a pine box
I lost my arm of joy, you the air you made chuckle
      with extreme folly.
You created with the flying élan of a trapeze artist
framing an Anglo-Saxon-jointed old barn
      into a Viking ship,

but when you descended in chemical melancholy,
even underground Orpheus couldn't flute you up
      from those hell swamps.
The last week you sent me your soul in a letter
of sorrow and confession. I failed to guess
      the German poison pills

you would swallow to end torment. "I love you"
were your words in Houston in the den.
      In our last phone call
your low remote voice still usurps my fun companion,
leaving a razor in my heart. I steal your eyes,
      keep only a shade

of you, an eyebrow of light. I need you. In my lungs
your shadow breathes. You lost the air,
      I my arm of joy.
Come back. Too many of us, hunted by time,
have descended early underground to perfect
      their memoirs through me.

SISTER

My sister, don't be blue. I don't know how
to send a voice to you that won't be pain
    in your wilderness.

You are remote from your pleasures, those ghosts
in need of real clothes from Bergdorf Goodman
    or even Target

to give you pep and bump you into laughter.
The blue demon has lingered long.
    So I am rushing

a fax to Houdini to rise from his trunk
in the Hudson waters to swim up just to you.
    Tease him in French.

Dear sister, let's hire a troop of magicians
to combat the night, find a deft Mexican muralist
    to color away blue,

and seat you in cold sun splashing the moon
on our German cottage, and a remote meadow
    where we trespassed

Swiss law and walked daffodil happy. You a child
and your bulldog barking around your ankles.
    I'm calling, leaving

messages, and ask the night of bats and blue fog
to end for good and for your bouncy soul
    to doll up again in brightness.

With Zo in the Botanical Wood

Zoë, we are not Russian but you and I
like to eat sack yogurt made by a lady
from the ballet-set city of Saint Petersburg,
and each time the wide-eyed peasant
offers us black bread and honey,
I say *spasíva* and we pick a lily

but not in the botanical wood
since here we gaze and gingerly drink
the beauty of names: a pepper tree,
a New Zealand rimu red pine,
a New England creeping maidenhair
or a Japanese waterfall where

we step and get wet. How can love
dance overwhelming from daughter
to her acrobat child? You are fable,
and the painted crow in the meadow
talks like a teacher. You respond
with the alphabet (you know its black

stars), and with wind on your neck
you say, "That's enough woods. Let's eat
some black bread and honey." But
the gate is locked and we're stuck alone.
I take your hand and we float over
the botanical mountain, eating yogurt.

THE LOST SON (LUKE 15.11-32)

We were two sons. Father gave me my share
of wealth and soon I gathered a few clothes
and books and took a ship into the glare
of Paris where I spent my loot on booze
and women, and one night of revelry
I got so stoned a thief came to my room,
bagged everything I owned in sheets. With glee
he tapped downstairs and fled. I felt no gloom
and never wrote my folks until I starved
in Spain. By then my father died, and I
came back to search for him. He saw me far
away from where he lay and called, "I carved
a cloud in here for you." "Make me your slave,
I've sinned," I moaned. "Take me from sun." But he
said, "You my child were dead and now you are
alive," and kissed my face from his dark grave.

GOLD WATCH

Dr. Sigmund Freud cures cases of hysteria,
sexual timidity and stonebelt depression
    by dropping words in a well

and letting his patient pull them up from memory
filed below sight and sighs, but not below
    heart, a poor heart invisibly

assaulting mind till it too breaks into madness.
Maybe I can cure my heart by writing down
    a terrible event that doesn't

even have the clinical discretion of hiding
in the unconscious. Out of flagrant lethargy
    I let my father's magic watch

get lost. That sin gathers energy as I age
and zooms back, a boomerang. I can't quiet
    the chaos. In 1922 Mother

gives my father a solid gold Waltham pocket
watch. When you open the first panel
    of the codex, it says in

elegant cursive: *from Blondie to Bob*. No one
calls mom *Blondie* but my dad. They are
    young and, from a picture

on the grass, they are dressed to kill:
suave, handsome and happy. After Father bolts
    out of existence to live

as a Chagall stained-glass portrait in my soul
whose glass eye always turns back to him,
        Blondie gives me the watch.

That watch—with its ancient gold hands moving
around its own planet as slow as the sun
        inching across a Castilian

sky in dead summer—I hold in my hand
and I look though its crystal face and below
        I feel his heart pulsing:

"It's me, It's me, It's me." The gold watch
like Sappho murmurs: "Somewhere someone,
        I tell you, will remember."

One afternoon in a Midwestern mall I pull
my wallet out of my tight front Levi pocket, and
        my wallet snaps it out

onto the floor. I take the dead movement
to a repair shop. Then phone. "We are waiting
        for an organ donor

and we're confident." I phone again. "Nothing yet."
Months pass. I call. The shop is gone.
        I get an address and phone.

Disconnected. It is worse than I tell it. My
delays were awful. Tomorrow and tomorrow.
        I let it disappear

as his presence leaves my hand. Worse, I buy
a rusty old pocket watch, merely gold filled, without
        inscription. I want to

replace the splendor of that precious slender case
and diamond jewel wheels and pearl eyes
        that torment me more

than ever. My watch and chain to dad are gone.
I keep them equally lighted in my heart's eye.
    Whenever I have done

something awful, despair at new passivity
or lose another member of blood, I still own
    a memory of chain and watch

keeping me sane, evoking a laughter
of walking down a primordial path
    in tropical Tabasco. I was only

fifteen. I'd have you for three more years
on earth. Blondie and Bob, hello, I'm older
    than you whom I love

and ask you not to forgive my disrespect
for a holy machine that married you in time.
    Your sorrow about me keeps

us all young as avocados on a twilight tree
in Provence. And since you're here, I hide
    the lead hell I'm used to

and chattering pages you never saw. Here are
lost years, a clump of gray hair and a triangular
    kiss of thundering gold.

Morning

Morning

Open your eyes and unfold
the black cloth fully and stretch it
open your eyes wide fix your eyes
concentrate concentrate now you know
how the black cloth is unfolding
not in sleep nor in water
nor as when eyelids close wrinkled
and sink slanting like shells
now you know how the black skin of the drum
fully covers your horizon
when you open your eyes relaxed like this
Between the spring equinox and the autumn equinox
here are the running waters here is the garden
here the bees bumble in the branches
and buzz in a child's ear
and the sun there! and the birds of paradise
a huge sun bigger than the light.

—George Seferis (1900–1972)

IKON

When you open the chapel's old door, Miryam,
captured by time, sits darkly with her son,
her baby with great eyes, in the center ikon
whose linear severity has survived theft and years.
Mother and child look terrified with love.
The eye star on the ceiling says eternally hope,
but the marble gods (below the Greek sea
splashing up to the glittery whitewashed chapel)
taunt the grave mother and her fated child
who wait desperately in candlelight, still in paint
on the rotting ikonastasis, still in flesh
kissed slowly into oblivion by the faithful.

                              Pigádi Vathí, Sífnos

The postman in love

I'm walking the circumference of our island,
carrying the breath of the postman who is young,
    only seventeen,
when he dies inexplicably in the garden
with a love letter pinned under his cap.

Inside my life watch an eye still winks
to see the postman while his corpse hears the bells toll
on the minute from echo mountains.
The old ladies and I eat a big salad of tomato and cucumber
    in olive oil for him,
and the sky opens,
turns mauve and expands unaware of its new desolation.

The mourning doves sing to the young postman
only seventeen years when he fell.
I have no love letter for you pinned on my shirt.
We are lost in our arms inside our whitewashed rooms
    over a ravine of rocks.
We have breezes in our lungs
but I envy the sweetness of the young postman
who sang island songs gravely and died in the garden,
sweaty, with a coarse bag of rosemary and salt
    to give the forlorn.

COMPANIONS OF LIGHT

On a dirt road from the island's mountain town
with its round white church and town hall clock
to a lone village now almost abandoned,
I fix my eyes on jasmines hanging over the stone wall
around some interior garden.
                              A crooked arch
shadows and cools the wrinkled eyelids of the cobbled street.
I stop and look at the ashen mountain
and back to holes of grass and a delicious honey blur
        standing everywhere.
The black cloth of mind falls away, and sheep seem to fall
back over the horizon just below the hermitage and Makários,
its one kind lecherous monk, lying in his robes,
chattering to himself on his cot.

Cloudy ships rock like slow whales going nowhere
        under a family of clouds
and through the holes in jellied clouds to the optic nerve
the jasmine petals glisten. They are letters of light
now perfectly visible and unreadable to a blind man
whose dead eyes look through gray wrap-around glasses,
who I remember is me,
who through the aqueous nothing in his sockets
imagines that winter is a July afternoon and a dolphin sun
        greater than light.
And this happy face with a black lens behind the iris
(the mad happiness is unreasonable)
smells every color of the floppy white shapes on the wall.

Zo near a Sífnos monastery

I'm sitting in a sketch pad while my son
Tony is drawing me in a Sífnos café,
and Zoë, already five, is making books
with tales she paints of dreaming clouds
and princesses hanging onto kite tails.
She dives into the sun on byzantine waves
slyly kissing the day's blue cheek

before a rose moon rises from the sea.
In the monastery chapel are phantoms
and varnished ikons of brown and silver,
breathing incense and the smoke of
skinny flaming candles. Frowning idols
of apostles and armored angels fade,
kissed away as healing gods. The blond

pantocrator—the fierce messianic Greek Jew—
walks along the dock near the church
to see something of his world. In the café
I'm sitting in a picture and watch my Zo
delighting the sea into her orange truck
while through blue windowpanes grave
big-headed saints stare from their wall.

VAGRANT

If I had not been a half-ass scholar (in Indonesia
    the taxi driver called me *guru*),
I think homeless would be a proper job for me.
I follow the way now from month to month,
changing beds. I don't want to be a vagrant
yet you see me going out, hopping from door to door,
asking alms, a stranger at home
with blank windows in a desolate neighborhood
where I stroll in light too bright to raise my eyes
above the children's hopscotch chalky on the sidewalk,
their drawings grinning at my happy ruin.

DRIFTING

After being kicked out of my fetid hotel
    and finding another
room with a sink on rue du Cherche Midi,
    it's celebration time
on a pale evening in slummy Paris. We go
    from café to café.

A friend sets up his tooty harmonica
    on his guitar,
fussing forever over them until at last
    he sings in
his invented Russian that drives me
    wacky. At dawn

we end up on a nostalgic breakfast bench
    at Les Halles,
sipping onion soup where I share
    my portion
with a flashy Jean Gabin-grim bandit
    recently discharged

from Devil's Island. *J'adore la musique,*
    he says. I'm in awe
but my disgusted companions
    have had it.
They flee. The skinny thief shows me his
    discharge papers

before he pillages me. Then I take
    the métro
to a public shower, and bus on to
    the Citée Universitaire
to black market the last few dollars
    shivering in my pocket.

In the morning I go to the Bon Marché
        to buy raw cotton
I sew into sheets for my humiliated bed
        but the concièrge
kicks me out anyway, indignant, her hands
        on her fat hips.

CLOUDY SUNDAY

Cloudy Sunday, you are mist like my heart
that always lives in clouds amid the blur
of being. On Tuesday the doc cut apart
my eye and slid a new lens in. What were
faces are now mud clouds. The cornea jell
is cloudy and like shaky jell I stroll
around the neighborhood in shades. I smell
the lumps of dark but dark befits the soul.
Sitting at Gaylords with a pad, I think
on paper so when light has formed I'll have
a picture of our bodies. The shroud
will drop. A memory face will be live ink
I see across the table. Now, I live
in dark, a blindman reading a black cloud.

Wartime Café

Often in Buenos Aires during the dirty war
I am translating sonnets of Jorge Luis Borges
who has an apartment on la calle Maipú
right across the street.
Blind he no longer sees the page
but in the unanimous night he repeats his own lines
with the sonority of calm thunder.
Normally we walk to the Saint James Café
on Corrientes to have our breakfast,
his place for a chat about the enigma
of Alice's first word on ascending from her hole
or how an almost fatal fall on the circular stairway
in his building led him to his first story.
On these long mornings
we sit with coffee and corn flakes
where the great mirrors show his white collar,
his head and disfigured eyes
and his black and impeccable suit.

With the Blindman

Thirty years blind. Finally he can't write by hand.
He signs his books in undeciphered cuneiform
and daylight enters his brain as yellow fog.
Sunday morning and we stroll to a book store.
By nightfall a taxi strike, too late for buses
so we have to walk, making Borges happy.

It's a bad evening of the Dirty War. We talk
about the savage ambush. Police tipped off,
waiting. Courtyard of corpses. We walk the city
from Palermo to Maipú, from midnight
to daybreak. When the *astuto* wants to delay
arrival, he sticks his cane in a *dim* hole

of the broken sidewalk. "It's like my face,
cracked," he insists. And pivots round it.
"Dim," he says. "We have no Old English word
like *dim* in Spanish, but I keep to my tongue."
"Did you ever see one of your outlaws
in action?" I ask. "Yes, up in Jujuy, near Brazil.

I was very young, and I went up there I guess
for linguistic reasons. I wanted to hear that mix
of Spanish and Portuguese. And a gaucho,
a black man, pulled out a pistol and shot
someone; then slipped his gun in his pocket
like a handkerchief. He kept walking as if

nothing happened." We near the flat on Maipú
where he jiggles his keys a long time. "Here
in Buenos Aires, my city, I am lonely. It is my fate.
And so I dream." The big bedroom, untouched,
was his late mother's. The blindman sleeps
in a tiny room on a cot good for nightmare.

On the First Day

Uccello

Al primo chiaro Adamo sente
il canto nero del uccello.
La sua paura no intende.
Quando è stanco canta cucù
l'orologio fino del corpo.
Quando è fermo non canta più.

Bird

At daybreak Adam hears
the black song of the bird.
He doesn't catch her fear.
When tired she sings cuckoo,
the body's delicate clock.
When still her song is through.

—Guglielmo Granaio della Petra
(1527–1561)

IN THE BEGINNING

In the beginning the life watches on the wrists of living beings
    measure that turning of time and of now
and twilight and twilight and the blackness.
By daybreak these inhabitants have bodies and consciousness
and see that it is good and they are in time,
and some of them weep on the ground
and would disappear from time as disappearing dust
    floating out of time,
and they are terrified and eager to form paradise and God
and God tells them to live and God tells them to die
and they are happy and with God
and some are not pleased with God whom they have made,
and some are found and some are lost
and a multitude of lonely inhabitants stand on the earth
    and think of their fragility
and in their loneliness look through telescopes
and in microscopes they look for a sky below their feet.

And while they choke from labors on the heating globe,
straggling through gravity to remain erect,
these lonely inhabitants see the solitary planets of desert,
    ice and terrible gases,
these dead children in the wilderness of space,
rolling overhead around their mother sun dressed in fire
    and piteously remote
from our cool drop of star spinning in a ring of air.

Only earth is a blue residence with carbon and oxides,
only earth grows a whale and leopard, lily and oak,
only earth holds the multitudes of breathing minds
residing here to eat and defecate and bloom.

ADAM THE SURVEYOR

Poor Adam is busy surveying the garden
and its infinite corners and its walls crooked like a London alley.
He has lost track of time, and worse,
he lost his Elgin under a tree of woe and joy.
Yet his watch would have misled him
with its circling hands never pointing to cruel eternity
but to himself a slave forever in the garden.

Young red Adam of the earth keeps busy and is nervous.
Eve has already tasted knowledge
while he is the dull worker of Eden's soil and grains.
Eve discovers fire and love in her thighs
and the wings of the tongue,
and she is good and gazing over the near wall.
He is about to crack.
The farm mule can't stand plodding God's vast meadows
     another second.

Adam throws his meticulous chart down on the dirt
and up springs a wind chiming: Scab of Eden, blessed stooge,
     fool of God,
and the slave of God catches on
and he looks at Eve, surveys her carefully like a panther loose
     in a temple,
and he kisses her breasts and immaculate belly.

Soon the two have risen beyond the hands of Big Ben.
They are gone to their own pasture high in a sphere of sun
     whose flame is tasty,
where their love and slumber are the color of milk.
Earth Adam and blossom Eve sleep in each other's arms.
Then back in rude time they wake with a memory of galaxies
     around their necks.

The prison gate of God's Eden is open.
Walking in the dark they are naked-eyed, condemned,
and perfectly deep for the long cold road.

AENEAS

In blazing Troy he lifts his father on his back
and they escape over the dawn hills of Ida.
Now after wandering Africa and the sea for seven years,
Aeneas enters the underworld to see his father
whom he embraces but he touches shadow.
His arms find only themselves and his despair.

Yet Virgil is deeply wrong. His creations rebel.
In death the father Anchises is alive and busy,
not merely a ghost of darkness waiting
for his son to descend. He has his own farmlands
and slaves whom he remembers through the son
and the fleet ferrying them all away from Troy,
and there is more than the escape.

There, long before the fires ravage Troy,
the father is walking in his coastal forests,
ordering his foot soldiers to gather wood and weapons
for an early march. And after these early tests of prowess
        and adventure,
of warrior and son routing ordinary enemies,
the old phantom of a man, still with all his senses,
recalls his young companion, how he loves his son
so obedient to his own heroic hours,
how the robust Aeneas once carries him to safety
yet then deserts him by remaining up in sunlight.

AFTER THE CRUCIFIXIONS OF 4 BCE

*And his despised corpse will be left unburied on the
road for all to see.*
                              —Isaiah

In Israel after Herod the Great dies it is chaos.
Roman soldiers plunder the treasury of the Temple
and Essene Sons of Light rebel, giving Rome a fit.

The emperor has had enough. Though busy
minting silver coins of himself as the Capricorn son of Apollo
(Apocalypse mints him as the Goat-Horned Dragon)
the divine Caesar Augustus keeps his Pax Romana
by sending in two legions of swords
under Quintilius Varus who blotch the sands of Judea,
crucifying two thousand rebels.

The body of Menahem lies unburied out in the street,
a criminal for all to see, his corpse pierced with knives.
The Sons of Light find him three days dead and rotting
in a Jerusalem alley,
                              their forgotten messiah.
Dead he lies in the street and nobody dares come near.

VIRGIL

Virgil the Roman poet is deathly sick in Athens,
but hangs on, believing in his epic,
for which he must still write six chapters.
In Greece for a few days, Augustus orders Virgil home
and the two friends set out together.
The feeble poet breaks down
in the hot port city of Brindisium. There he dies.

Poor troubled Virgil had ordered his literary testator Varius
to burn the *Aeneid* if he failed to make Rome alive
where he could finish his work,
but his patron the emperor Augustus will suffer
no prideful stupidity of fire, and he is law.
The *Aeneid* is saved
and Aeneas (unlike his creator Virgil) reaches Rome.

On the way the hero of Troy descends into hell
where he hugs the shadow of his father.
No one is there, only a voice. Aeneas is furious,
but the scene contrives to make him helpless
before his father's shade.
The humiliated soldier is confused by his author's heartless
        evocation of the encounter,
and in frustration turns his head to Italy,
to the tomb of Rome's marble poet
and, given new life by the emperor to have his story told,
Aeneas curses the mist greening Virgil's dead lips.

Seder in One of the Odd Rooms

In a small room above an eating place,
hunted Yeshua and friends plan to drink wine

and eat the matzoh one last time. To face
the tales making him real, he will recline

at supper with his favored student. Far
north in a lone room in Florence, Fyodor

epileptically scribbles a dwarf star
into an idiot's eyes and lets him soar

over Saint Petersburg, sleeping on clouds
of poppies. A small room saves us from harm

in Lapland darkness where a nun and I
work in a winter sardine factory

with other young poor souls, and we stay warm,
kissing in sheets against the time of shrouds,

but in Jerusalem, Roman troops upset
the Pesach. Sworn to keep their secret banquet,

Yeshua orders: Go out of the city,
find a man carrying a jar. There we will meet

upstairs in a small room. There we will share
the pascal lamb. A cup of wine I'll pour,

giving my body and blood. Keep this memory.
We'll talk and ponder death and slowly eat.

YESHUA BEN YOSEF AT THE STAKE

When they spike him and raise the T-cross,
he screams. Then flies buzz around the rabbi's
nose and none of his friends dare speak out.
All those hours of pain weaken him
with the insufferable iron in his ankles, hands.
He shouts to God, "Why don't you come?"
The soldiers laugh. "Let Yahweh save you,
Jew!" Pilatus is bored. He's crucified so many
of them. Miryam of Magdela alone
is brave enough to climb the knoll and sponge
his mouth. She kisses his dripping wounds.
Seconds left. It's Friday and the Seder. He'd be
with friends. Yeshua dies. The temple curtain tears.
Yeshua ben Yosef is tossed into the regular
garbage pit outside Yerushalayim, into the fire
of Gehenna, a black grave or a pearl
in heaven. The true story and man are dead.
The burning rabbi cannot open his eyes.

OPHELIA SINGS OUT

Goodnight, sweet ladies.
The rosemary remembers

how her clothes spread wide
and the mermaid drowned.

A skull had a tongue in it
that once could sing.

Now open to the underworld
in my gravedigger's gloves

I snoop again below
in the wet underground

where Ophelia sings out
of exquisite compassion,

down in the filth, beseeching
her return to lucky day.

SPINOZA IN THE DUTCH GHETTO

Smoking his pipe he takes a beer with friends
at a close eating place, or back at home
and shop he grinds the glass to make his ends
meet needs. Lean life. Then drops down to a dome
of Latin thought and pen. Why ask for more?
He trades his work with Leibniz who is keen
as calculus to open every door
and wheel him into Germany to teach
and make him known. The lens grinder has seen
that greater world only in spheres that reach
the end of mind, and all mind plus all sphere
is God for him, a take that by itself
could set his life on fire. Baruch is not
a scrapper but all peace, all sky, no fear.
A Spanish Jew safe on his Lowlands shelf,
a bird on the North Sea, floating in thought.

BAUDELAIRE SUFFERING WINTER

Sick Baudelaire suffers through winter, calls
his Catholic soul, and overhears his whores
in sensual jewels. A tenebrous clochard sprawls
along the quay at night, hiding his sores
and hunger under a stone bridge. The cold
soot paints the Paris afternoons with ice
in rusty pots of cabbage soup for the old,
who soon will die. The grand dandy of vice,
living on opium and Poe, will live
a few more seasons. *Hear, my love, O hear
the gentle strolling night,* he sings in his
last poem. Escaping from the syphilis
and stroke, he tries God's ink to write and give
his boredom the black ecstasy of fear.

MACHADO AT HIS WINDOW

In this small city of Baeza where I guard a memory
of first seeing young Federico, up from Granada
with fellow students and maestro don Luis del Julio,
my heart is turning about a woman who fled
into the terrible sunset with its drops of blood
and absorbs her and my dream of us walking
chastely among the poplar trees until the path
also falls into the fire. God, who is never on earth
or in the skies, strikes me again, stealing

my daydream. I have buried too many friends
in the yellow earth, saw the gravediggers
let the coffin drop in the hole under horrid light
and heard their gloves clapping before the thud.
In war Madrid I am seized by a second memory,
austerely real, of young Federico walking
between rifles through his streets of Granada.
That is a later sorrow, but here in fertile Baeza
I dream of harsh Soria where I found and lost

Leanor. The road, as in a film going backward,
turns around and we, side by side, are coming
to the warm river. There, our landscape
blooms late in adolescent northern spring.
The horse gallops between lightning bolts
to the mountains. I turn to her, she holds me
among a swarm of shadows. Her pearl earring
sighs in my mouth, and we are lying
in a bedroom perched on the wharf of nightmare.

Daybreak with Jean-Louis Kérouac

♪

Never expected Jack to show. I'm eating supper
with Gregory Corso in a lonely blue Italian joint
in New Haven. He is coming up alone to read

his poems at Wesleyan. Bragging about Jack,
Greg gets mournful as if Kerouac had spun off
the planet. I say, 'Look, Jack's not a corpse.

He's alive, knocking it out. What kind of shit . . .'
Corso, the straight pin of the gang, lets me have it,
'Ginsberg sleeps with everyone. Allen, poor Allen,

he's just a whore. I'm the only straight dude
who's ever slept with Jack-o'-Lantern. We're tight.'
Corso's proud of being top gun with Kerouac.

Jack stinks out loud with whisky, but off booze,
he's really low key, gentle. He's a timid man.
On the weekend, Greg shows. He's come up

from the city with a tired wobbling bum wearing
a black ratty raincoat hugging his ankles,
a black fedora and shades . . . *Hey, that's Kerouac!*

You gotta be kidding. Drunk as a hog, his feet
made of cotton, Jack's smiling a lot. I ferry him
to Olin Library and present him to Professor Greene,

expert in Christmas carols. Jack asks Greene,
'What are you teaching, sir?' 'Shakespeare,'
responds the patrician teacher. 'D'yuh like

Shakespeare?' says Jack. 'I love Shakespeare,'
states the professor. 'Overjoyed, Jack shouts,
'I love Shakespeare too!' And he grabs his new

friend's cheeks and slaps a wild kiss on his lips.
'I've read your books,' says Greene. 'I like 'em.
Where can I take you?' The scholars skip off.

♫

In the evening, Corso stuns me. 'Are those tramps
going to beat me up?' 'You're crazy.' But Corso
won't read his poems. He raves about his hero

William Burroughs, whispers a chapter from *Naked Lunch*
and we're transported to jungle rapture and shots
of heroin Burroughs sticks in the ass of a Brazilian boy.

After a discourse on love, Greg and the gang of pals
Jack came up with from New York jam into a side room,
and Jack is sober and describes his dawn climb

up Mount Tamalpais north of the Golden Gate.
Jack is impassioned. 'I climbed Tamalpais.
I got to the top and beheld daybreak. I saw satori!'

'You saw bullshit!' Corso throws in. 'I saw bullshit,'
Jack confesses. He surrenders. A buddy knows I'm nuts
about everything Greek and puts on an LP

of *hassapiko* from Asia Minor dens. Jack tells me,
'Let's dance.' We squat, arms locked, and we're doing
the butcher's dance strict and low until Zen daybreak.

LEOPOLD AND HIS LEPERS

Except in gospels and paintings I am ignorant
of lepers until one afternoon I walk
through banana fields near Mayaguez and climb
a sun-heavy road to a leper colony
commanding a hill over the Caribbean.
I find Leopold up there who had iced
his cousin Bobbie Franks from Chicago in '24.

Thirty-six years later, released from Joliet Pen,
for his penitence he chose to go far
and live among the pestiferous. The lepers smile
when I walk up to their cabins and clinic.
Short Leopold, ballooning in his white jacket,
takes my hand and we blab all day long.
The devil is human. His grand hobby

is birds. Earlier he tried the perfect crime
and mathematics. Done with that, now
he tends the bodies of the dying. Bald, in peace
and meticulous, Nathan, into his seven years
in an isolated camp on Puerto Rico's mountain
for medieval demons, cheers and instructs me
about health. Roly-poly Nathan introduces me

to the clinic doctor, his Puerto Rican wife,
who tells me about new medicines, and Nathan
goes on and on about migratory birds
on their way to the poles, and about a blind
disfigured cardsharp lady who outwits him.
Leopold, murderer of a now forgotten young
cousin, is busy soothing the cursed lepers.

OF JULIO WHO ALMOST KILLS ME

I wonder if I can forgive Julio Cortázar
who conspires and almost crushes me.
He does it by writing a mysterious story
I am reading in a Buenos Aires subway,
standing, rocking a bit in the clanking car.
It is not "End Game" but a fantastic tale
of two houses and a railroad car with a rider
who never arrives yet is forever a woman waiting
like me in the train, not wanting to look up.
Argentina. Every day during the Dirty War
is better than the next. I've always liked danger
in demoralized lands with autocratic regimes
and the comradeship of persecuted writers.
Here under Perón and his vigilante thugs
in plateless Fords halting at midnight houses
to help an artist disappear, I am excited by
Julio, the Argentine short story magician, and read
lost. As we move around a curve, I lean back,
feeling for the car wall when a middle aged lady
says quietly, *La puerta está abierta*— The door is open.
She saves me. Julio is alive, and if he'd killed me
I would have preceded him into shadow land
where I'd have time to read forever, with proper glasses.
I forgive Julio. Grimly, with no one to warn him,
the multiplying white cells will crush him early.
But down there, alert with his shadows, I see him
unwilling to forget his eternal readers. With only
a pencil he dreams up novels and fantastic tales.

Twilight

Memento

When I die
bury me with my guitar
under the sand.

When I die
among the orange trees
and spearmint.

When I die
bury me, if you wish,
in a weathervane.

When I die!

—Federico García Lorca (1898–1936)

WHEN I DIE BURY ME WITH RAW ONIONS

When I die bury me
with raw onions and garlic
so I can keep healthy,
and a digital phone
to apologize to those
I hurt by dying,
to those I hurt by
having been around.

And don't forget
to call. And if you
have old equipment
and can't get through,
with your learning
stoop on my grave,
dig a small hole
and I'll be waiting
for your whisper.

And through the ceiling
of garlic-smelling earth
I'll dig back up to air
and press my lips up
to greet the impatient
who love me, whom I love,
whom I leave helpless.

LAPLAND

The roots of the earth protrude
down into the pinegray ocean
and up into the glacial snow.

There are not many fir trees
as we push into the unreal
north. We are beyond the green

and on nude scrubby earth again.
Here where snow yawns into the
sea, and air is clean like fish,

distance and form and seasons
are more true than the odd boat
or village. Time. This land is

dream—planet where almost no one
is—or if real, then quick cities
south are dream before the slow

iceland. At night sunshine floats
on big mountain ribs of snow;
gulls cry and cod run in the ocean.

OCEAN SPEECH

The ocean feels too much sorrow to say hello
to me drinking hot chocolate in Vera Cruz,
only a few meters from her winter hat of foam
babbling by my sandals in waves of tears.
She wears a jacket of figs and drifting garbage
and a hundred years of roses whose smell covered
alleys and newspaper stands in the tropical city.

There are many rich upstairs widows mourning
officials from San Juan de Alúa and far Puebla
and hut widows mourning Indians in white pajamas,
passing their lives as companions to ox and hoe
and old widows waiting eagerly for the ocean to move
out of her pocket down their street to enter them
and drown them in dignity next to a riotous cantina.

Here, down from the Autónima, I came a while
to know a woman in this tin roof tropical city
by the ocean who fusses. Now with my hot chocolate
favored by huapango dancers and Maya gods
and workers on the oil docks shipping black gold,
on this hot night of ocean groaning in the engravings
of Spanish slaveships slipping over throbbing hair

the ocean and I talk heart to heart about what
to wear on Sunday morning and of street orphans
who sleep in mounds on the bad avenues
by opticians and sad venereal disease clinics.
Though hard to catch her plashing words,
the ocean voice amid her continents slows down
to a soft roar in a cup of chocolate on my table.

CASTILLO NEGRO

Por la ventana redonda
del cuerpo, castillo negro,
el ave de la negrura
ya sale buscando el día,
volando bajo el desierto
a un secreto río oscuro
donde una perlita huele
a eterna lata del sol.
Busca la sombra del mar
en donde rondan los peces
y una pestaña de arena
donde su perfil descansa.

Pájaro de la negrura,
¿qué es este grito penoso?
¿No ves la sombra encendida
que alumbra toda la playa?
Queman las velas del cielo
en aire y sol bondadoso.
El pájaro no responde
por ser animal agudo,
y busca siempre más luz,
aspirando al mediodía.
Espera cambiar su cuerpo
por el brillo de cenizas.

Un pájaro calcinado
vuelve a la negra ventana.
Antes era palomica
con alas de blanca paz.
Ahora vuela invisible,
rayo de luna borrada.
Ansía cual niño ciego
un farol en el castillo.

Fuera luce la negrura;
dentro, un amor vagabundo.
Mas sólo el amor clarea
en el castillo la sombra.

BLACK CASTLE

Through the round window
of the body, a black castle,
the bird of the penumbra
wings out seeking the day,
floating below the wasteland
to a secret dark river
where a tiny pearl smells
of the sun's eternal tin.
She seeks a shadow in the sea
where fish swim their rounds,
and an eyelash of sand
where her profile can rest.

Bird of the penumbra,
what is this harrowing cry?
Can't you see the flaming dark
bleaching the entire beach?
The sails of the sky burn
in generous wind and sun.
An animal of cunning,
the bird does not respond,
and seeks ever more light,
aspiring to the noon.
She wants to change her body
into the glaze of ashes.

The calcinated bird
returns to the black window.
Once she was a pigeon
with wings of paper peace.
Now she flies invisible,
a ray of erased moon.
She longs like a blind child
for a beacon in the castle.

Outside a blackness glows;
inside, a vagrant love.
But only love brightens
the shadow in the castle.

BLUE TIBET IS VERY HIGH

Blue Tibet is very high. Fog hangs on yellow fields
  of mustard plants.
  Hard to breathe
at the top of the world. In far thin air
some leather-faced nomads tramp by in black rags.
Up here in rooms in Lhasa
  the nuns are tortured, the people in terror,
and in ribbon villages the sole monasteries not in rubble
  are ghost cloud mirrors
of packed highland summer snow.
The skinny police are walking in gray cloth bags.
Along the hills, strings of prayer flags flutter in winds,
  defying guns.

WAITING FOR THE BARBARIANS

> *And now what will we do without the Barbarians?*
> —C. P. Cavafy

The emperor has no brains. His ministers, mentors
and minions know the condition of our leader
and administrate his mind with blatant tact,
and no one, not even his cowed opponents, breaks
the hypocritical code. The aura of silence about
the emperor's mind is mandated by expediency.
No child calls out: *The emperor has no brains!*

And we seem lost. Maybe the word hypocrisy
is severe to type a man who stumbled to his throne
on an orange, and fear makes him popular.
As regional crown prince he broke a record
for executing hooligans, each time blessing God
for his harsh mercy. The popular fears stays on.
We're united. Would you be profiled a traitor?

The emperor depends on the holy barbarians
who march in multitudes, who tremble the streets
down to their tar intestines. These ancient furies
tear their hair out and rip bras and blouses
from their bodies. Our leader breathes soft at barbaric
hoots. They cry *Idiot!* They shriek *Face of Satan!*
Our monarch is pleased their wicked ways are loud.

Our people love a dumb emperor. He's one of us,
a common man with vices who likes a pistol,
a guy talking back to barbarians. He will bomb them
before they smash us. He smiles and looks frightened
yet it's sweet to be an emperor and host premiers,
athletes and heroes, and not live in a sewer
but in a great white house circled by big cannons.

There is melancholy in our land. And bad news.
Russians claim barbarians live only in the Caucusus
or have facelifts and own slot-machine parlors.
Are there no wild beasts in a desert once Eden?
Our emperor's men have gone underground
in panic but send up blueprints to create
a goat-horned dragon roaring over the ocean.

Our mindless Caesar lies on the ground and weeps.
It is sad to live under a subnormal emperor.
We are tanking and he bumps along in his golfcart.
The barbarians were a solution. Another winter.
What can we do? We're obedient as Mongol ponies.
The emperor's minions haunt an underground city,
run secret courts and e-mail God for our next step.

We are waiting for the barbarians. Our emperor
has memorized his speech. He has no brains
but our child comes home from school, saying:
God will protect us. Our bad one is cunning.
Maybe our barbarian will not blow up the world
or fling us all in prison. Our sad one smiles.
There is a terrible melancholy in our land.

Hanging from Spikes, Dropping to Earth

"He must be thirsty," someone in the crowd
is saying. "You think even he's not scared?"
another says. He whispers from his cloud
of agony. "I'm fading!" He too cares
to live. Who doesn't? The trapped jumpers soar,
some holding hands. For love? In terror? They
can't last in the building a second more
of smoke and flaming clothes. Hung from spikes he
too wants more breath like every visitor
to earth. The sheep are leaping out of hell,
hurling from windows, plunging down the sky
to nothing they can see. Last breath of air.
They pole cheap wine to his lips. He cries. "Why
have you left me?" And sags while jumpers fall.

IF GOD HAD AN APARTMENT

Whether Deity's guiltless
My business is, to find!
　　　　　—Emily Dickinson

If God had an apartment down the street
where Oakland cops and a Black Panther friend
are singing hymns, I'm sorry but I wouldn't eat
a sumptuous meal with him, this guy who'd spend
your soul on hope. I can't forget his past,
those freaky power trips, always for praise
and faith. Consider Avram whom he asked
to kill his son Yitzhak—who'd never gaze
on sun or kin again. Yes, God canceled
that sacrifice before the knife found heart;
worse he spared only Noah and band but killed
all breathers on our earth. He's been a fist
of shame, an SS type. If God were smart,
he'd take that knife—penitent—to his wrist.

The eleven commandments

1 I am the Lord and I brought you out of Egypt, out of the house of slavery. There are other gods. But you have one God. I am I.

2 Make no idols. I am the maker. Those who create art will compete with me. You may worship them and lose me. If you make idols I shall punish your children for three and four generations. If you love me, since I am a lonely God I will care for you for a thousand generations. Love me, obey me. No statues.

3 In argument or court or the market, do not use my name for influence. I am a private God. I intervene when I wish, but you are not me. Do not stand in the pulpit babbling as if you are God. If you pass for me, I will erase you like an idol.

4 Shabbat is mine. I labored to form letters and place them on cloth of black fire in order to read those letters as words and speak creation. I created twice. Once in six days. And then all in one day when I created a garden with Adam and Eve. Two cosmic efforts. Remember what I did. It was for you. Remember that you were a slave in Egypt and I delivered you. Now pause, enjoy, even meditate. I command you to loaf. If you are not lazy and joyful on your day of rest, I will tumble stones on your heads and then you may remember our labors. I have blessed Shabbat.

5 Honor your father and mother who, like me, are your makers. Dishonor to them is abuse of me. If you honor your father and mother, they will like you and forget honor and walk with you in gardens.

6 Do not kill. I kill. Time kills. Disease dismembers and kills. Do not add to that misery. If someone tries to kill you, whisper something quickly to me. Unfortunately, I may be absent. I tend to many and tend to be on line elsewhere. But all my work does not give you license to own guns or kill. Burn the weapons, big and small, of killing. Have a good life.

7 Do not sleep with the spouse of another. There are many to sleep with, including your solitude, which may delight you with never imagined feasts. The world has a mountain of partners. Why look for trouble? If your heart is beating with desire, remember me, your Lord, who has everyone and no one. I stand alone in the sky.

8 Do not steal the shirt of your kin or even of your enemy. And worry about it, since even I who know all do not distinguish between stealing and enterprise. Even your prosperity may help if you steal from your neighbor, and your poverty may help if you steal from your cousin. Look into the mirror. If you see only two figures, you and your heart, if your hand does not shiver, forget this commandment. If you steal and your hand does not shiver, you are destined for great power.

9 Do not rat. A silent face is diamond. If you rat on friend or enemy, a circle of smoke will turn you into a rodent, not a hare, but a rat. Better to be a siren, a singing Josephine who comforts her fellow mouse folk who live in shadows and pipes, than to rat.

10 I am the jealous God. You must not be like me. I possess the world, and its people die and wives and husband, slaves and oxen and neighbors all become dust and I possess nothing of them. You will have nothing if you do not learn from death, from the dust maker, for your soul, if you covet the things of others, will turn deadly. You will not look in yourself where you are a sky infinitely deep and with unending aromas. Do not be jealous like me.

11 I am a weary God, who has not been listened to. That may be just, since I have taken to long absences. My plate is empty. Do not quibble whether I have been good or bad, whether my commandments are good or bad, whether I am or am not. If you want a good life, I tell you to listen to my commandments. Or do not listen. And if you cannot listen, hear your soul. It is there, asking you to loaf. And when you have truly seen your soul and believed, and are comforted by its vastly intimate rain forest, enter her and forget me.

DANCING WITH ELECTRONS

When I pop out of my file and shut down
    unwillingly, meaning crash
forever, don't forget we've e-mailed
          intimately and must keep

it up. I'll hear a fly buzzing in my brain
    before I fall, and will change
my address to will@eternity.com.
          It's easy. Or you can try

bill@hunger.grave. I will read you.
    I may be dust or ash
but my invisible electricity will be dancing
          with electrons to spare.

Do I freak you out? Have faith. Not in miracles
    but in titanium Macs. My switcher
spans life and death, earth and the template
          of heaven. And if we're trashed

hit lunar@hope.fly. Then a new generation
    of friendly operating systems
will zero us though unbound space where we'll dance
          on both sides of Mars.

SECRETS OF THE LONELY

I wear black support
hose because a young
ophthalmologist on call
almost killed me with
horse serum. Mistake.
He thought I had lockjaw,
a just call, since my
friends tell me lockjaw
would give me measure
and tune my big mouth.
Later Dr. Wey killed
himself—not for giving
me a shot of death—
and my still swollen
ankles and I remain
deeply sorry for helpers
whose ways are fatal.

I was a hair from zero
time. Then abundant
cortisone saved me from
Dr. Wey's poison needle.
We the lonely are many,
crank or cow, and hope
for mercy from a contracting
cosmos on the night when
all we regulars and suicides
lie together and party
till the cows come home;
then breakfast on lilies
and loaf our afternoons
in obscure but cheerful

cafés serving us for twelve
billion years, feeding us:
we sparkling sub-particles
of blue horse, lily, and lover.

TALKING TO AN ORANGE

Pardon me—don't listen to me—
for living. Why? Do I ask for too much
    that I care to be? Orange,
you exist and end up being an ecstasy
    on the tongue, the aim
of our wakening at dawn. Must you, orange,
    disclose your identity card
and your decomposition? I am always
    surprised that chance
has me born and dying on this planet,
    that I speak to you with desire
to be an unconscious peel or a calm sphere
    with electrifying juice
to bloat the belly of the daybreak sun.
    I loaf in an airless mall
of souls, and below an orange moon
    I am when nothing
persuades me that I am. I watch a voice
    performing in my mouth
a necessary illusion. Orange, with no
    cares about being,
you look at me from one unblinking eye
    in quiet non thought
in a perfection a Buddhist would sit still
    a year and never reach.

Russian and Spanish jail friends

Most of my poet friends—with them
I live most intimately—know
a jail or die in one, their phlegm
goes dry, they disappear. I go
to my room, read them out loud.
They hear. I kid myself. Miguel
dies of TB, his chest a cloud
of liquids leaking out. The hell
of Osip ends when he is shot,
warming the Russian ice. Juan dies
in a monk's cell. In black night he
has slept with secret sun. I'd be
with them but can't, so read. Time dries
on my cot. But I want their lot
and strangely live their deaths. Why not?
I love them. Why not be happy?

FEELING HIS MIDNIGHT ARM

Especially after midnight when we walk
around the city—Borges loves to stroll
and spin around his cane and stop to talk
and talk, and never stop—he spends a whole
hour comparing Hopkins to his Milton. No
taxis, another strike, the hospital
once more filled with young *montoneros* who
fight the police and lose and we are full
of midnight books. We move again. This team
of arms. He's blind and eighty and I'm half
his rascal wisdom. All this spoofing in
the night. Then dawn informs us: we must laugh
back to our flats, our night vanished again.
I grieve. Borges' dead eyes are fixed in dream.

Past Midnight

Summer Night

It is a beautiful summer night.
The tall houses leave
their balcony shutters open
to the wide plaza of the old village.
In the large deserted square,
stone benches, burning bush and acacias
trace their black shadows
symmetrically on the white sand.
In its zenith, the moon; in the tower,
the clock's illuminated globe.
I walk through this ancient village,
alone, like a ghost.

—Antonio Machado (1875–1936)

EVENINGS IN BUENOS AIRES

I relish every night in Argentina
where crazed Isabelita shrieks her dream
in the Plaza de Mayo. Perón's last niña,
she is the boss whose butchering regime
kidnaps at night. The dirty war. I go
to hear her speech with a photographer,
a Syrian friend. We leave for home and row
our night of love while nightly massacre
plays out in the *athletic clubs* where youth
are tortured, drugged, dumped in the Paraná.
I stroll to breakfast at the chic Café
Saint James, loving the city, though the truth
of *desaparecidos* paints each gray
night bomb with raw, screeching Caligula.

Snow in the Dakotas

This afternoon the Dakotas are shedding snow
again on Badland reservations and bleak hillocks
as I walk in the blizzard like a drunk drinking

spiked wind. The *Coast to Coast Hardware*
is a pleasant shock of heat. In my borrowed boots
I trail trucks and a limping cat and huddle

for a while, looking over a Sermon of the Plain iced
for followers, snow ghosts like me with my codicil
of heavenly words for freezing transcendence.

A shot of Sandman port before I sleep,
a mattress in the Dakotas where my blood asks me
to snore through bedless months (to sleep in my own

sheets is strange). Aliki lies in rhapsodic linen,
on rags of dream. We've had our gifts on earth.
Standby. I've flown here for a freezing teacher

unable to take food, my daughter near death.
In dim Dakota I follow a pickup home, a white night,
a star in my throat, and gales of snow and snow.

HER HANDS

When she was twelve she rode our rented white
horse in Vermont summer of secret walks
through the far field. There we climbed a low height
into our secret meadow where the flox
and birches spouted dreams. Now she's a thin
young woman with a profound Rilke sad-
ness. This autumn she couldn't drink a pin
of water, sucked on ice chips on our mad
drive back to the Mayo Clinic in time
to stick an IV in and operate.
Last week she was near death. Near the Badlands
my daughter is recovering, saved from
her clogged gullet. She swallows now. Her hands
are young gazelles leaping while she sleeps late.

FULL MOON OVER A TWO-NOTE MAN

Full moon, I am a two-note man. I toot
on high or low. Tonight I'm low in bed,
and low despite the wonder of you, brute
glow ball bounding through the window. Sour lead
winter moon face, last night you stood over
my car racing beyond the exit on
the South Dakota interstate. Earlier,
I walked shivering through night-bleak Vermillion
under your hardware smile. Soon mud, then spring.
I am a funeral bell, low high, a bag
of coffins prancing under your dark lips.
I can't drag up to drink or write. The sting
of mercy pounds in me until I sag
absorbed into your mouth and blazing hips.

NIGHT OF AN EXQUISITE MORNING

I had a narrow room on the roof
of our poor pension in Mexico City.
Write me if you're alive. I'm ashamed.
You came to solitude. Your name is fragile.
I knew you vaguely at the school
and you suggested this house. I'm there.
At the table we often eat together.

In the evenings I read in my white cell.
At nineteen my thighs shoot out heat
like the lightbulb alone above my bed.
At dawn I see Popo who is smoking slowly
like the owner of the kiosk at the corner,
seller of oranges that hide in their center
a moon green with hot plains of Vera Cruz.

I hear a plash of water drizzling just
outside the window. The Indian maid
is taking a shower. Her nakedness makes
prince Popo blush. She is my age. Quickly
she dresses and leaves. I'm stretched out
on my back, eyes tranquil, and the door
opens. Someone else has climbed up

the ladder to the roof. It's you. You let
your skirt drop, lift the sheet and lie on me.
You eat my mouth and sit down on
the tree that doesn't know the rain
in the center of the orange. In sun
we join, we sleep. Then you get up and leave
the air. If you're alive, I'm here on the sheet.

A CZECH WAKES AS A COCKROACH

I have become a book. A wretched book.
I read and write, glaring at a dead page.
That's me. Papyrus in my heart. I look
at a lost mummy who has lost its rage
for sucking hope, all that Platonic air
I carried in my youth, the floating form
above the air, from cave to blaze. It's fair
to type me. I agree. If you deform
me as alive, I'll bitch. I am a dead
Coptic scripture and don't decipher me.
Please leave me cold in clay where it is nice
and peaceful. I'm an ingrate in my bed,
who won't get up to piss, who loves the spice
of brainless grief and anonymity.

OPEN THE WINDOW AND LET THE NIGHT AIR
COME IN WITH ITS PERFECT MEMORY OF STREETS

On la rue Jacob the basement windows are evening bookstores
with a few ruby-colored titles on cream books by French masters.
Jewels, they glow under glass, Gide and *le mot juste* of Flaubert.

At midnight the volumes are still lighted. One store has a poem
by Henri Michaux signed by the author while taking experimental
drugs. Hot water in my room with a shabby red rug, by my bed

I keep one condemned work I love, a gift from a young freckled Jew
I fail to pursue: *Les Fleurs du Mal.* The cursed poet's perfections
are as clean as Racine's alexandrines but quirky and salvific

for a raw fanatic student who is too broke and flawed
to finish a program. I don't fret. I have a life before me.
Maybe I will paint, go to the Beaux Arts and stay in Europe,

shock an English princess by stripping when she visits my atelier.
Maybe I'll end up in a Spanish whorehouse looking for a sermon
in carnality. Maybe I will climb to my bed with rare books

from a small bookshop, let them heat my sheets, and cart them
around the Mediterranean in a sailor trunk to Tangier where
I can print poems in ruby type and watch them tremble on vellum.

With a lone folder of special edition pages meticulously perfected,
maybe I will find the steam to push through my life of imperfections
that sit acrimoniously here, messy as they squirm and glare at

drying blueberries or me through my enthusiastic arthritic fingers.

BEAUTIFUL MOVEMENTS

The old IRT sub rocks dad and me
all the way down to Maiden Lane for just
a dime. Crammed on yellow seats, carefully
among fedoras and windy howling dust,
dad reads his paper, I a comic book,
using our time. Up on the seventh floor
dad keeps modern Swiss watches with their look
of Cycladic figurines. He is the author
of their ticking beauty. I love my dad.
We eat at Schrafts. I follow him out West
when New York cracks. His watch is spinning; when
the jeweled movement fails, death is a sad
and soundless stop. Though he let go, my pen
and ears and hollow arms keep him from rest.

Rooftop

If when my father climbed the iron stair,
folded his coat and neatly set his hat
on top, and neared the guard wall to the air
of Colorado spring, and squinting at
a circle in the street that would bring sleep,
he saw a child or heard a crazy fight
over a baseball card, or if his leap
would have smashed me posted under his flight
plan, if a girl had cried, if a Ford truck
had howled up to his ears, then the squat wall
would have spun him around, me at his side,
hugging him down the steps. He'd never fall.
I tried to come on a red-eye plane stuck
in storms, which hit the tar just as he died.

MY FAMILY IN BRIGHTNESS

My sister and I are the only ones
of the original five alive today
in our family of brightness.
Mother I took through Central Park
in 1955 to the operating room
in Beth Israel uptown in Manhattan.
She lay bright for a few days;
came the knife, and we couldn't say
goodbye. Father is closer to me

because he left more violently,
jumping from a Colorado rooftop,
like Zero Mostel, and his sorrow
and our love stain my heart;
and my brother, consummate fabbro,
hurt and slipped almost silently
out of being with soporific tablets.
This afternoon my sister, who won't be
okay after her electric shocks, sent

this note. "I miss you! I started
to write a note to Mother and Dad
and didn't know where to send it.
I am taking treatments that affect
my memory. Where would you
write to them?" They are powder
underground. This is our history,
a family of five, who shared air
on this planet for a bright while.

COFFINS OF BLACK

A child's death cannot be explained.
I wonder why the lovely French girls
I saw in a Catholic hospital in Périgueux
lay unconscious on their beds
their faces gazing up at the ceiling.
The young faces seemed healthy,
a cancer raged inside.
They were not in pain, they were fully still.
In white gowns they lingered
in sun passing through the glass walls.
In stunning beauty and peace,
they ceased breathing and went
where no child should go,
where no child should go.

THOU AMONG THE WASTES

Time is a ferryboat lumbering one way
for each of us, yet floating endlessly,
porting new customers for a quick lay.
Shakespeare in sonnets cursed the husbandry
of hideous time which, cultivating death,
defaces us. Yet ferries hold their course,
ferrying you, allowing me a breath
of life, until we drown below the floors
of rock where no time shines. I wonder how
I've lasted while the young collapse. William
himself died young but not before he got
his feather pen to decorate a bough
with wrinkled suns against the cold. I am
his ship of wormy time, blessing his rot.

First word

At Bowdoin I began to know the bleak
stone Upjohn church and isolating snow
on my black morning tramps down to the Greek
diner for breakfast. I was young to know
puddles of sorrow; at sixteen and raw,
I didn't have the pot of fire Hawthorne
found in the woods, yet winter nights I saw
out of his window into his forlorn
Puritan burning in her village heart,
combating God and governor for light
of antinomian darkness and the dread
constructed butterfly of art. My part
was set. I feel these fifty years tonight
of old, bleak papers. Dark fires till I'm dead.

Dawn Café

Paris at Night

Three matches one by one lighted in the night
The first to see your full face
　　　The second to see your eyes
The last to see your mouth
And the full darkness to remind me of all that
As I hug you in my arms

　　　　　　　—Jacques Prévert (1900–1977)

NIGHT WATCH

Night watch. I look at the face
of the movement. Too dark. Yet cool air
    from the window
hits my back. I can't let life go to sleep.
In the kitchen lies a round loaf of rosemary
    olive bread.

I slice it, pour Metaxa brandy. Eat,
drink, then go back to my head where
    on a mountain
of revelation a busload of angels in blue
jeans whistles down from Venus.
    "Come up.

It's hotter on the love planet."
I have no fable to cool off regret
    when my night watch
tells the pain, and solitary I grab
and find nothing in me. I'm stuck.
    Then leap

off the building of me to you.
You are there coloring this desolation
    with a bit
of orange, a drop of honey,
and love stronger than a big vial
    of iodine.

ON THE SILK ROAD

In China we are in a great public room.
We shake hands. You faint in December
and now our mattress lies in the kitchen
        in my Friendship

Hotel flat, and we dine with old foreign
ideologues—not many local Maoists around
by now—and I don't take off my life watch
        in the shower

as I scrub your belly, surprised to feel hot
water. This morning we're packing light,
and secret down the back stairs of
        your Peace Hotel

(we're watched), and turn anonymous
in the buoyant crowds on Wangfujing.
My novelist friend Wang Meng is out
        of prison (sixteen years

exile in old Xinjiang where the epic poem
is strong) and we bus out to Kashgar
on the Pakistani border and Uigur women
        wearing big river pearls

in low desert villages. In the outdoor market
labyrinths along the Silk Road, we cool off
with watermelons. A steel Mao bust
        and a mosque eyeball

on the skyline. A silent war of Turk
and Han. On our last afternoon in the mist
of a Muslim graveyard on the border
        mountain, we walk

among the graves with their goat horns
on small white domes. We stop, then ramble
among ancient peoples, hawk and caravan:
    inventors of sky and road.

CAFÉ DE L'AUBE

Je dors et déjà vis demain. Lundi
sera. Mais non, c'est un beau dimanche matin
    négligent

et je danse avec Dieu, une belle femme
qui me dit bouche à bouche dans mon âme
    le secret

banal de ma confusion et pourquoi
je ne peux pas dormir, pourquoi obligé
    je me lève

du sommeil pour te parler dans le noir,
des heures avant le café de l'aube
    qui me sauve

sans doute. Je me trompe. J'embrasse
la bouche de Dieu. Elle est douce et ne
    me méprise pas

que je meurs sans espoir. Elle m'assure
que sa présence n'est pas nécessaire
    et je l'aime

dévasté par son dur éloignement.
J'ai froid. L'hiver est sur mes genoux. Chaude
    elle sourit.

Dawn café

I sleep and already live tomorrow. Must be
Monday. No, it's a beautiful negligent Sunday
    morning

and I dance with God, a beautiful woman
who tells me mouth to mouth in my soul
    the banal

secrets of my confusion and why
I can't sleep, why I feel forced
    to get up

from sleep to speak to you in the black,
in the hours before the dawn café
    that saves me

undoubtedly. I kid myself. I kiss
the mouth of God. She is soft and doesn't
    blame me

for dying without hope. She assures me
her presence isn't necessary
    and I love her,

devastated by her remoteness.
I'm cold. Winter lies on my knees. Warm
    she is smiling.

VINCENT ON THE TOILET WALL

If you paint me you paint the illusion of an illusion.
—Plotinos

On the Bake House men's room wall,
    to the left of the toilet,
hangs a framed Van Gogh poster of almost
    good color called

"Field of Poppies." When I go there
    I look at it with faith
and astonishment that earth possesses
    a rug of poppies

mourning the vanished and filling the living.
    Vincent even loans me
his poppy moon with its mad Ocean
    of Storms nightly

consuming me with its own rain
    of orange bullets
hitting the wall and scorching the window till
    I zip up and leave.

IN THE BROOM CLOSET

In the broom closet of my head
my prayer is a nightmare galloping
on a meadow round and round.
Tonight I'm ready to cry out
but the lord God has no time to answer
the phone or my old-fashioned
letters sent to heaven. I e-mail
my missile of despair to God.com.
If the old testy man responds
it will smell of a slaughtered goat.
With nothing fixed, brooms on the floor,
I go on muttering to the leaky faucet.

MEMORY HOUSE ON PLATO STREET

In the small rented house on Plato street
I stumble through the Greek newspaper,
then stroll through the alleys of Kefissiá
on narrow sidewalks crowded with cars
(the lamp posts have posters with pictures
of leftists in jail or exiled on prison islands)
and descend into a bistro to hear Psaháros
sing us and collapse us into cloud soul.
Smoky but not jammed tonight. He sings
his gravelly "Agonía, agonía." Earlier I walk alleys
of Thessaloniki, sapphire of the Jewish diaspora
where the Goths put up a wall and gas
seventy thousand Spanish Jews still with keys
from Toledo and the court of Alfonso el Sabio.
Who remembers a slaughter in north Greece
where the ancient inhabitants are stoned
in the central square and trucked away
to special gas trains? Today I straggle among
the dictatorship colonels (they house arrested
Ritsos and Seferis), and in this taverna
where a few couples have finished dancing
to the love songs of Manos Hadzidakis,
I forget, sip retsina near the floor lights,
sit mesmerized by Psaháros singing agony.

THE SHTETL GHOST

He was lost and he has been found.
"Parable of the lost son"
—Luke 15.26

You are poor and father's dad and never come
down from Boston to the city to meet me
and so I never see your face.

I miss you, Zeda, my friend. I'm not only
sentimental but feel your anonymity
as if I lost a brother

(it happened). Is your black maid now
your wife? Bits of gossip about the widower.
Where are my black cousins?

You must be a short tailor out of Poland.
At Krakov I saw Copernicus's glass eye
that beheld the night,

and like his planets you revolve around
the sun but beyond my sight. Close to Krakov
is Auschwitz where

I looked at baby shoes and poor suits
you might have sewn together had you not taken
a steamer in 1887

to Boston, coming not as a Pole
but as a Yiddish Jew swallowing red borscht
and meats fried in chicken fat.

Were you mean? I'm caught between you
and father who left the house and the sixth grade
in anger. You come alive

for a few seconds in a Sunday phone call.
You hit on dad for a hundred bucks. He shouts,
"The only thing you ever gave me

was your belt!" I didn't expect a fight
I care for you, Zeda. Am not lying. I'm glad
you are not a poet

with your pockets stuffed with words.
You make vests and coats and we chat
about the art of cutting cloth.

You squeeze my hand and invent me.
You are Sancho Panza snipping sharp words,
scissoring me this evening.

I'm your age. Your voice sticks my finger
like a sewing needle to keep me around.
We know the loneliness of work.

You say, "I cut, you write. Some are dogs,
some are birds." I say, "You're a cloth ghost
I am seeking in a grave."

"No, Billy, we've wasted lots of time
but now my grandson has come. We can keep
meeting in some old book."

Blind date

Nightly I slip in bed and take a chance
on disappearing (I won't even know
if I wake dead), but it's a ball to dance
away in dream, not hearing as I go.

WHEN I DIE BURY ME WITH LIGHT TICKING

When I die bury me
with light ticking
in the vapor sun
below the waves

when you come.

Since that won't work,
let me circle,
a crazy slopping around
a lamp post

when you bury me.

Wanting you always,
I'll become you
below the waves
with light ticking

when you come
to bury me.

Train to Paris

To Kydro

I'm waiting
to see you, offer
gifts for a
safe arrival.
Much labor
in voyage,
and to you
I say, I
am coming.

—Sappho (612? BCE)

GIVING A WATCH LIFE

Repair me, watchmaker. Insert your tool
into my chest, its oscillating spring,
my heart, and screw the spindle in the jewel
and the frail balance wheel of steel will ring
in silence while its tense mainspring will store
my spunk to last a day. Then close the case
and I'll hop downtown to a lover. Poor
in discipline and peace, now in my race
with night, I'll own another day to tick
and tick. But fix me just a bit. I want
my sweet to feel my movement, touch the dial,
to open me and poke around. Then sick
of perfect gears, she'll blow on dust and haunt
my parts and kiss me out of time a while.

A FOOL OF SIGHS

I am a sighing man, or worse I moan,
playing the weak man in a Russian tale
where everyone is poignantly alone
and paralyzed but witty, and I fail
like Chekhov's dreamy characters who stall
and can't reach Moscow. My heart ticks away.
Now paralyzed I mutter and recall
a convent room in Spain, a jasmine day,
how I was crazy for her lemon thighs,
for someone happy to play woman God
and burn my balls, for mystical San Juan
consumed in holy lily, body lies
and sexual dream, for memories of a dawn
of lips . . . A fool of sighs I grab my rod.

LONELINESS

I am an old guy on the stage. Are you
an actor too? To be a star is death,
the pits (that's my fond script), and I'd be through
by now, a theater poke before a breath
of poetry slips in. While poor Sir Fame
goes touring Mars, glowing in underground
caverns of clapping ice, I live in shame,
thank God. I'm here to belch, to pound
my brains against a rock, bumbling with cheer
of youth, hoping for parts, facing a life
of vulgar impulse. No regret. My wife
is solitude, who hides me when I fear
I'll flop naked before the ghosts or lie
in heaps of verse and sigh and sigh.

PS I LOVE YOU

My father left me love. On the shelf four
silver goblets. Jack tells me I should take
them. Jack, dad's friend, says there is nothing more
to carry home. Oh, three Van Gogh prints ache
in their frames! I'd sent them from school and he
had them dazzling the white walls. I let
him down. That's how you feel, sad and guilty,
when your dad dies alone. I don't forget
a single second in the New York hotel room,
talking all night, cot next to cot, our eyes
the only souls in town for us. A week
went by. A call. I came too late. He lies
this evening in his Colorado tomb
while in our every dream we speak and speak.

SECRET FACE OF LOVE

The secret face of love changes her name.
Was it Lily, God or Francesca? Plato gave her
a good face, spoke a symposium about her.
Chaucer's nun with eyes as gray as glass
wore a coral rosary about her comely arm
and a necklace of green beads dangling
a brooch of gold, saying, *Amor vincit omnia.*

Some whisper whore at her or say she's dead.
She is an insomniac. I am her inconstant
scribe since my passion changes. I hurt her
and her face suffers. So does mine.
Her face is always with me. She is my father.
I call her woman, first love, old love, new love.
I touch her unknown face. She's in the papers

but no nuclear threat. Do not bomb her. We
are lovers. Day moves to dust, dusk to night.
It is dark. She is the one I've always loved,
here with me now. Sleeping. We are wed,
illegitimate, warm flesh. A lily is a day of
eternity. In oblivion she is tender in my arms
and in my sleep, I gaze at her gazing face.

WINGS OF THE MORNING

If I take the wings of the morning
and dwell in the uttermost parts of the sea
or knee my way up from cloud to cloud and find the mist
    won't hold me,
or plunge into hell and make my bed of poisons there,
you are also there,
my echo, and I your echo, you who frame me with the echo
    of the first morning of being,
who knit me out of the earth which in secret you mix
    with my blood.

If I take the wings of the morning and fly toward your hand,
you receive me a monster and child in the pit of dream
where I ponder implacable extinction with no escape
    into light,
and though you are nameless we shadows converse
and go to villages, wake early on a secret meadow
where we climb to a morning mountain of secluded high grass,

And when every joint screams, when I stumble alone
in the dim prison of me with no old key from Toledo
    to give false hope,
when there is no one, none, when zero is my frame, even then
    in extreme silence
I take the wings of the morning and hang onto impossible winds,
and wherever I drift you are with me.

FEELING YOUNG

I feel so young because I am still where I was
and looking for a supper with a secret reader

and so I'm a youth in Paris with a sheaf of lyrics,
some about to show in a new yellow mag

put out by Bernard Citroën, a Dutch poet,
who passed five years of Occupation holed up

in an Amsterdam basement. By chance I pass
an afternoon with an elderly formal gentleman

who shows me his books. To me he is myth,
but with exquisite melancholy Tristan Tzara

says he is forgotten. The rebel is all soul today;
earlier the Resistance and hiding from the Gestapo

in cave rooms under Bonaparte and Boule Miche.
A year later, walking in Monasteraki, I see Kimon

all smiles. He sits me down with the poet Seferis
in a gray diplomat's suit, fresh as a windflower

on his Anatolian coast of Byzantine and Turk
and French crusader. For him the war was exile

in Africa. We spend our morning talking London,
his translators. I see him pleased that one so young

as me found his book a year ago in Paris.
These are sun days. Though I step toward night

without morning, I am still where I was,
twenty-one in bright Athens, looking to share

a supper, worried but cool on Greek fava beans
and yogurt, and the privileged wait of youth.

SAILOR OF THE STARS

I dreamt of being a sailor of the stars,
of floating amid the dust of galaxies
with a flashlight as my only instrument.

Into the border of a dream I went perfectly
awake, eyes open to the interior sky
and took off from a frozen cornfield

and rose, at first diving up, then drifting
as if on a cosmic iceberg. No purpose
but the flight up and quickly I was born

into a nothing atom without a name,
autistically free of self, and in madness
I dangled by new moons with faces

of broken playing cards and a hideous flash
of jungles on dwarf meteors and bonfires
incinerating death. God drinking fine port

tipped his cap. Soon I sank to childhood
and went almost daily diving from a board
into chlorine water at my school or the Y.

I dived high into ice peak fear and bliss,
paused, spun, descended near the killer board,
and sharked safely in till my feet felt tile,

and then, blind to gossip of levitating Freud
or astronauts for real or even the great
voyager Juan de la Cruz who in darkness

rose Plato blind and dumb into the sky
as woman merging with the lover God,
with no Flash Gordon as a model, suddenly

my soul turned around when in Colorado
in May daybreak when medieval Spanish birds
are said to waken and scribble songs

through space, my dear father desperate
to end his time, swan dived from a roof
and whirled down to the street and became

the sailor of the stars below the earth
where I search in moon and dream, dead awake
or happy in illusion that we're out tramping

another hill in Mexico where we wandered
once like kids before the fall. I leapt once
out of a small plane above the Connecticut

River, and I was scared, but I shared seconds
with my sailor dad who chose his mystic leap
to crushed oblivion. I still dream of being

a sailor of the stars or trekking by the sun
and have a few years of sailing over meadows
earth has given me. Let me float a while.

A child looks ahead to ponds in the sky,
to mountain plateaus where naked bodies
hug sweet air, to stars of impossibly huge

fiery gas bombs that even glass spaceships
only photograph, there I dream of floating
with star sailors and my lost dead awake.

AT MY FUNERAL

I take a seat in the third row
and catch the eulogies. It's sweet
to see old friends, some I don't know.
I wear a tie, good shoes, and greet
a stranger with a kiss. It's bliss
for an insecure guy to hear
deep words. I'll live on them, not miss
a throb, and none of us will fear
the night. There are no tears, no sad
faces, no body or sick word
of God. I sing, have a warm chat
with friends gone sour, wipe away bad
blood. And sweet loves? I tell a bird
to tip them off. Then tip my hat.

WHEN I DIE BURY ME IN FIRE OR EARTH

When I die bury me
in fire or earth,
I don't care. Or best
forget the soul's

insult, who is death
who cannot learn
to take a powder.
Let me keep up

my life watch
with you. Love, a ghost,
tangos in and out
of graves and paper.

the body's rhyme.
When we can't dance
and someone dresses
my unticking corpse,

please chop me up
for a public hospital,
letting organs
waltz to the song.

In my solitary hole
drop in my wristwatch,
nothing else. Oh, a daisy
and an extra battery.

MEMORY IS MY SHIP

Memory is my ship

I like the sea its sky of rocking water

the green clouds under the sea

where my lovers gossip

about me how I am always

a clock pausing in old days

a rock conniving on Mars

Memory is all we are

I love memory in my bed

the voices haunting me

below the sea I wait joyless

for silent night in the port

for my ship to go where

memory was to be again

in bed with voices now at sea

It's true I was really wild

but will I be more gentle

when they and I are only sea?

TRAIN TO PARIS

In the night boat-train
from Le Havre to Paris
I sit by a young woman my age
who is from Carpentras,
daughter of a Breton sculptor,
and we are heartsick
after our three hours. We know
we'll never meet again
except she will remember
me, our hands, and I her,
though I learn in 1956,
four years after our night,
she died on a Paris street
when a car crushed her
from behind. In her grave
we are sitting cramped
but our conversations never
run out of gravity.
Down from the train of time
(I piss on time), we endure as souls
and our scandals create us
on the platform kissing.

Notes & Acknowledgments

"Virgil." While in Athens for a few days, Augustus orders his friend Virgil home and they set out together. The poet breaks down in Brundisium (Brindisi) where he dies.

"Spinoza in the Dutch ghetto." Baruch or Benedict Spinoza (1632–1677), the Dutch pantheistic philosopher, lived quietly in the ghetto during his short life, dying from tuberculosis probably aggravated by his inhaling glass dust from his scientific lens grinding. Despite radical ideas of God that earned him excommunication by fellow Jews in 1856, he felt free and safe in the Dutch ghetto and selected not to take a professorship in Heidelberg. Shortly before he died he began a critically enlightened translation of the Hebrew Bible. Though close to mathematical Descartes whom he translated, he does not split mind and body which for him are distinct qualities of a single substance he calls God or nature. God is nature in its fullness, suggesting, perhaps by coincidence, the gnostic pleroma (fullness) that represents the gnostic deity. Spinoza's friend Baron Gottfried Wilhelm von Leibniz (1646–1716) was a rationalist philosopher and mathematician. Three years before Newton, he also invented infinitesimal calculus (1684). As a logician and metaphysical thinker he shared with Spinoza the notion of the universe divided into rational monads. For Leibniz each monad is a distinct immaterial universe with self-consciousness, arranged in an infinitely ascending order. His optimism led him to a satiric role in Voltaire's *Candide*.

"After the 2000 crucifixions, 4 BCE." Herod died in 4 BCE, after which there was chaos, rebellion against Rome, and the crucifixions. Menahem, meaning "comforter" in Hebrew is the Essene messiah. In the Gospel of John "the Paraclete," an epithet of Jesus, meaning "comforter" in Greek, is modeled after Menahem and Isaiah's prophesy of the earthly messiah. In Apocalypse (Revelation), 666, the goat-horned dragon, is usually said to be Nero, but in two Dead Sea Scroll hymns the linguistic and historical evidence points to Augustus, who appears on his own coins as "Capricorn," meaning "goat horn." See Israel Knohl, *The Messiah Before Jesus: The Suffering Servant of the Dead Sea Scrolls* (University of California Press, 2000).

"Seder in one of the odd rooms." The hunted Yeshua is Jesus in an upstairs room at the Last Supper.

"Yeshua ben Yosef at the stake." *Yeshua ben Yosef* is "Jesus son of Yosef," *Yeshua* (Joshua) being short Aramaic form of Hebrew *Yehoshua*, *ben* is Hebrew for "son" (*bar* is Aramaic for "son"). *Prushim* is Hebrew for "Pharisees," *Miryam of Magdela* is "Mary Magdalene," *Yerushalayim* is "Jerusalem," *Gehenna*, Hebrew for the place of dead tortured souls, is sometimes translated as Greek Hades or Old Norse hell.

"Thou among the wastes." From Shakespeare's sonnet 12, "That thou among the wastes of time must go."

"Wings of the morning." After Psalm 139. For Charmaine Craig and Andrew Winer.

"Night of an exquisite morning" and **"Dawn café"** I wrote originally in French.

"Sailor of the stars." "Astronaut" in Greek means "star sailor," that is, "sailor of the star." The poem is for seven lost sailors of the stars (2/2/03).

"Memory house on Plato Street." In 1492 the Spanish Jews (Sephardi) were expelled from Spain. In the diaspora to Southeastern Europe, Holland, and Turkey, many went to Greece, hispanizing the ancient Jewish population. During World War II the German army built a ghetto wall in Thessaloniki, where most of the Jews lived until they were sent to their death in gas trains and the camps. In a well-known scene in the grand plaza in Thessaloniki, the quisling premier ordered thousands of Jews to assemble with their belongings. They were stoned and jeered and then turned over for deportation. Jorge Luis Borges has a sonnet called "Salonica," about Jews still with their keys to their houses of their native Toledo. Toledo was the seat of the court of the Spanish king Alfonso el Sabio (1252–84) under whose reign Muslim and Jewish culture flowed into Western Europe. In Toledo, capital then of Spain, was the famous School of Translation where, among other works, Plato and Aristotle were translated from Arabic into Latin and Spanish, feeding the emergence of 13th-century humanism.

I thank Alan Michael Parker for his sagacious hand and generosity. For reading and shaping poems, Sarah Handler who saw, heard, and encouraged each incarnation; Mark Turpin who helped me to the dedication that centers the work; Joseph Stroud whose comments I cherish; Richard Silberg who sees star time in a poem; Elli Barnstone whose wisdom touched the book's tone and distinct languages. My son Tony tested poems, came up with grand solutions, ordered bad angels out and gave me measure and vision. My daughter Aliki labored over them with passionate devotion, ingenious artistry, and rejected the weak. She witnessed them again and again toward a final character and polish. Without her eye and voice, this collection would have been dim. For hearing them on the phone, Stanley Moss, Gerald Stern and Ruth Stone, patient and loving. For the Argentine composer Gerardo Dirie for perusing "Castillo negro" and the Italian scholar Massimo Mandolini Pesaresi for words on "Uccello" and the poet Guglielmo Granaio della Petra, ancestor of my heteronym Pierre Grange. For incising nine of these poems on steel plates set on wooden pedestals near RISD and Brown in Providence, my son Robert Barnstone. For their faith in receiving these orphans Steve Huff and Thom Ward. Thom met with and dressed each poem in his comments. Steve gave the collection design and the reality of print. Never before so much care and long joy.

Some of these poems have appeared in *The American Voice, Chelsea, DoubleTake, The Formalist, Harper's, lyric, New Letters, The New Yorker, The North American Review, The Northwest Review, The Pedestal Magazine, Pleiades, Prairie Schooner, The Red Rock Review, The Ryder, The Southern Review, The Southwest Review, The Times Literary Supplement.* "Our New York skyline in the 1930s, now on fire in September" appeared in the anthology *September 11, 2001: American Writers Respond* edited by William Heyen.

About the Author

Willis Barnstone, born in Lewiston, Maine, and educated at Bowdoin, the Sorbonne, Columbia and Yale, taught in Greece at the end of the civil war there (1949–1951), in Buenos Aires during the Dirty War, and during the Cultural Revolution he went to China where he was later a Fulbright Professor at Beijing Foreign Studies University (1984–1985). Former O'Connor Professor of Greek at Colgate University, Willis Barnstone is Distinguished Professor of Comparative Literature at Indiana University.

His books include *Modern European Poetry* (Bantam, 1967), *The Other Bible* (HarperCollins, 1984), *Poetics of Translation: History, Theory, Practice* (Yale, 1993), *Funny Ways of Staying Alive* (New England, 1993), *The Secret Reader • 501 Sonnets* (New England, 1996), *With Borges on an Ordinary Evening in Buenos Aires* (Illinois, 1993), *Algebra of Night: Selected Poems 1948–1998* (Sheep Meadow, 1999), *The Apocalypse* (New Directions, 2000), *Border of a Dream: Poems of Antonio Machado* (Copper Canyon, 2003), and *The Gnostic Bible* (Shambhala, 2003).

A Guggenheim fellow, he has received the Emily Dickinson Award of the Poetry Society of America, the W. H. Auden Award of the New York State Council on the Arts, the Midland Authors Award, three Book of the Month selections, and three Pulitzer nominations. His work has appeared in *American Poetry Review*, *DoubleTake*, *Harper's*, *The New York Review of Books*, *Paris Review*, *Poetry*, *The New Yorker*, and *The Times Literary Supplement*. His literary translation of *The New Covenant: The Four Gospels and Apocalypse* (Riverhead, 2002) was an April Book of the Month selection.

BOA Editions, Ltd.

AMERICAN POETS CONTINUUM SERIES

No. 1 *The Fuhrer Bunker: A Cycle of Poems in Progress*
W. D. Snodgrass

No. 2 *She*
M. L. Rosenthal

No. 3 *Living With Distance*
Ralph J. Mills, Jr.

No. 4 *Not Just Any Death*
Michael Waters

No. 5 *That Was Then: New and Selected Poems*
Isabella Gardner

No. 6 *Things That Happen Where There Aren't Any People*
William Stafford

No. 7 *The Bridge of Change: Poems 1974–1980*
John Logan

No. 8 *Signatures*
Joseph Stroud

No. 9 *People Live Here: Selected Poems 1949–1983*
Louis Simpson

No. 10 *Yin*
Carolyn Kizer

No. 11 *Duhamel: Ideas of Order in Little Canada*
Bill Tremblay

No. 12 *Seeing It Was So*
Anthony Piccione

No. 13 *Hyam Plutzik: The Collected Poems*

No. 14 *Good Woman: Poems and a Memoir 1969–1980*
Lucille Clifton

No. 15 *Next: New Poems*
Lucille Clifton

No. 16 *Roxa: Voices of the Culver Family*
William B. Patrick

No. 17 *John Logan: The Collected Poems*

No. 18 *Isabella Gardner: The Collected Poems*

No. 19 *The Sunken Lightship*
Peter Makuck

No. 20 *The City in Which I Love You*
Li-Young Lee

No. 21 *Quilting: Poems 1987–1990*
Lucille Clifton

No. 22 *John Logan: The Collected Fiction*

No. 23 *Shenandoah and Other Verse Plays*
Delmore Schwartz

No. 24 *Nobody Lives on Arthur Godfrey Boulevard*
Gerald Costanzo

No. 25 *The Book of Names: New and Selected Poems*
Barton Sutter

No. 26 *Each in His Season*
W. D. Snodgrass

No. 27 *Wordworks: Poems Selected and New*
Richard Kostelanetz

No. 28 *What We Carry*
Dorianne Laux

No. 29 *Red Suitcase*
Naomi Shihab Nye

No. 30 *Song*
Brigit Pegeen Kelly

No. 31 *The Fuehrer Bunker: The Complete Cycle*
W. D. Snodgrass

No. 32 *For the Kingdom*
Anthony Piccione

No. 33 *The Quicken Tree*
Bill Knott

No. 34 *These Upraised Hands*
William B. Patrick

No. 35 *Crazy Horse in Stillness*
William Heyen

Colophon

Life Watch, Poems by Willis Barnstone,
was set in Garamond fonts by Richard Foerster, York Beach, Maine.
The cover was designed by Daphne Stofer-Poulin, Rochester, New York.
Manufacturing was by McNaughton & Gunn, Saline, Michigan.

The publication of this book was made possible in part by the special
support of the following individuals:

Nancy & Alan Cameros
Peter & Suzanne Durant
Dr. Henry & Beverly French
Richard Garth & Mimi Hwang
Robert & Adele Gardner
Dane & Judy Gordon
Marge & Don Grinols
Kip & Deb Hale
Robert & Willy Hursh
Archie & Pat Kutz
Boo Poulin
Deborah Ronnen
Andrea & Paul Rubery
Sue Stewart
Allen Tice
Pat & Michael Wilder